The Writing House 1
Contents

CW00531564

All **Channel 4 Schools** programmes are subtitled on Teletext for the deaf and hearing-impaired.

We are always pleased to receive constructive comments and suggestions about both the series and the support materials. Please write to me at the address below.
Adrienne Jones Education Officer Channel 4 Schools PO BOX 100 Warwick CV34 6TZ

The Writing House and the Curriculum

Using the programmes

Each programme in **The Writing House** is designed to introduce children to a specific purpose for writing. The writing is explored and explained in its real context, then revisited by Mr Write and his friends who examine the structure and conventions of the texts as they practise writing. This format creates an ideal model for the teacher and children to follow in the classroom. It incorporates text-, sentence- and word-level work.

Using the Teachers' Guide

The activities in the Teachers' Guide are designed to consolidate and develop programme content, and to enhance children's understanding through class, group and independent work. They aim to support children's development as writers and increase their enjoyment of writing so that they become more confident and competent.

Each programme in the series explores aspects of the range of work outlined in the National Literacy Strategy, including labels and signs, rhyme, instructions, speech bubbles, characterisation, questions, retelling traditional tales, non-chronological writing, and fantasy story writing. Transcription skills are practised throughout, and the use of ICT is modelled and encouraged.

The programmes can stimulate discussion on the key topics outlined above. Through children's responses and comments, teachers will be able to identify individual needs and help children make links between what they know about spoken language and what they are learning about written language. Suggestions for discussion are made in the teacher's notes.

(T) Text-level activities

Throughout the series, clear patterns are presented for narrative and non-narrative writing. The text-level activities examine language features and conventions as well as the composition and layout of written materials. Suggestions are given for discussion and shared writing sessions in which children demonstrate and identify what they know already. For example, many children will know the structure of a narrative (that it has a beginning, a middle and an end), and through a variety of lively practical activities they can explore how narratives might be written. Non-narrative texts are explored in a similar way.

(S) Sentence-level activities

Children's grammatical awareness and their ability to construct sentences and use punctuation are revisited regularly throughout the activities. Emphasis is placed on practising these skills through purposeful writing.

(W) Word-level activities

The rich use of language in the follow-up activities is intended to engage children and encourage them to enjoy and explore the complexities of the English language as well as extending their spoken and written vocabulary.

Word lists are given as starting points for discussion and to help with spelling. Some activities are designed specifically to examine how words work: for example, the study of the composition of words through onset and rime, and the enrichment of language through synonyms.

Children are encouraged to use a range of dictionaries to enhance all aspects of their word-level work. Handwriting activities consolidate work on developing a cursive style.

Classroom organisation

The Writing House can support children's development as writers, both within and beyond the Literacy Hour, by building on and broadening their existing knowledge.

Television is a stimulating and accessible resource which teachers can use to model writing and to show the writing process in real-life settings. The use of video allows groups or individual children the opportunity to revisit extracts for reference and reinforcement.

Shared writing, where the teacher models all the elements of the writing process, is an integral part of most of the activities. This makes explicit the links between spoken and written language. It also serves as a model and resource for children's group and independent work.

The activities in this Teachers' Guide cater for a range of abilities and have been differentiated so that teachers can select those most appropriate to particular children or groups. Suggestions for groupings have been made throughout, but the activities can easily be adapted to meet the needs of the teacher and the class.

Activity Grid

Programme	Text (T)	Sentence (S)	Word (W)
Programme 1 **Signs and Labels**	signs and notices shared writing poster discussing scripts and language independent writing	capital letters upper and lower case commas 's' pluralisation	labelling 'CVC' words onset and rime words within words ICT handwriting joins
Programme 2 **Writing a Rhyme**	rhyming verse greetings addressing envelopes annotated frieze action rhymes	poem layout rhyming couplets proper nouns capital letters layout and design	spelling patterns shared writing common letter strings 'near-miss' rhymes compound words
Programme 3 **Writing Instructions**	language and tone shared writing composition instructions sequencing	full stops headings capitals and full stops shared writing story map	onset and rime letter strings 'oil' and 'eed' dictionary work alphabetical order lists
Programme 4 **Speech Bubbles**	story composition storytelling character profile shared and independent writing storyboard	capital letters exclamation marks speech bubbles speech marks ICT	phrases sound effects spelling rhyming dictionary handwriting
Programme 5 **Writing a Recipe**	layout and illustration writing a recipe non-narrative description invitations	abbreviations capital letters names and titles ICT asking questions	lists shared writing letter strings cooking verbs time adverbs
Programme 6 **Describing a Character**	poetry letters character study	character sketches abbreviations	verb-ending 'ing' adjectives
Programme 7 **Questions**	email pet survey recording data question and answer	question marks questions such as 'why?' composing questions shared writing	word chains phonic: 'wh' dictionary spelling
Programme 8 **A Traditional Tale**	storytelling drama and role play beginnings and endings retelling a story book-making	labels capital letters ICT	homophones 'CVC' words spelling
Programme 9 **Writing a Guidebook**	shared writing descriptions composition of books notices	descriptive writing shared texts capital letters ICT layout and fonts	spelling strategies adjectives phonic: medial 'oo' onset and rime
Programme 10 **A Fantasy Story**	story consequences story planning plot, setting and character shared writing drama	shared writing sentences punctuation tenses speech marks	handwriting labelling adjectives lists spelling features alliteration

Signs and Labels

Programme outline

In this first episode, we are introduced to the three main characters: Mr Write, who is better at magic tricks than he is at writing; Word Bird, the resident and very literate magpie; and Violet Plant, the visiting gardener who's brilliant with a computer. Mr Write needs to tidy his den because he doesn't know where to find anything. Violet introduces him to the idea of labelling. Word Bird shows us examples of signs and labels in the real world before Mr Write completes his writing tasks back in the house.

Before watching

- Discuss how labels are used around the classroom.

- What signs have the children seen on their way to school? What words and symbols have they noticed?

- As a shared text activity, make a word bank of 'tidy' and 'untidy' words – such as *neat* and *messy*.

While watching

- Stop the tape after Violet has shown her labels. How has she written them? Discuss what labels Mr Write needs for his den.

After watching

(T) Text-level activities

- Talk about the language of labels that inform, give orders, and warn.

- List all the signs that the children have noticed in the programme. Discuss logos, symbols, and slogans.

- As an independent or group activity, ask children to survey and list all the signs and labels displayed around the school. Ask them to note the variety of languages and scripts used.

  Use the information they have gathered as a basis to write a commentary that describes what Word Bird sees as he flies around your school. (Don't forget to include what he says in response to the 'cat'.)

Cat! Oh no, don't say that word! Shut up! You know it scares a bird!

- What signs – such as 'Welcome' and 'Please do not run' – do the children notice around the school? As a shared writing activity, ask the children to compose signs for the classroom – class rules, for example. Discuss the importance of using appropriate vocabulary, the need to be concise, and how symbols are sometimes used to replace words or to reinforce the written message.

- As an independent writing activity, ask children to design a litter poster for the school, or to design posters for a shop window of their choice.

  Encourage them to think about the size of their posters, the style of writing, and the use of capital letters. Use a computer to design and print their posters.

- Collect labels from packets and cans. As a class, read the different chunks of information given, such as the name of the product, instructions, and ingredients. Children can then try designing their own packaging.

(S) Sentence-level activities

- As a shared writing session, model the use of capital letters for names and titles such as 'Mr' and 'Mrs'.

- Focus on children's name cards to examine capital letters. This work can be reinforced through writing their names in saltdough, sand, or string. They can make a name label or badge for their friend.

- As independent work, children can match upper- and lower-case magnetic letters to make pairs.

- Make a list of labels needed for the classroom. Use this as a shared writing model to explain the use of commas used to separate items.

- As independent work, ask children to compile their own list of things they would label in, for example, their bedrooms. (The lists could run horizontally, with items separated by commas, or vertically.)

- During a shared writing session, discuss and demonstrate the use of 's' for making plurals (for example, 'pens', 'pencils'). Make reference to words that don't need to be made plural, such as 'scissors'.

Ⓦ Word-level activities

- Use the list of labels for the classroom to focus on spelling, capital letters, and handwriting. Give out the picture of Word Bird on page 24 for the children to label.

- As part of a shared writing activity use Mr Write's examples of label-making for words like 'pen' and 'top' to illustrate 'consonant-vowel-consonant' (CVC) words. Make explicit the initial and final consonants, accepting children's invented words when appropriate. Use the words to make a flip-over book, cutting each word into consonant, vowel, and consonant.

- Focus on the rhyming words used in the programme, such as 'book'-'cook', 'toy'-'boy', 'nest'-'best'-'rest', 'pen'-'ten'. As a shared writing activity, distinguish between onset and rime by collecting words with similar endings. Choose other rhymes, such as 'send'-'lend'-'bend'-'spend'.

- Develop children's use of 'words within words' as a spelling strategy: for example, 'spending', 'spend', 'pen', 'end', 'ending', 'in'.

- Play a game in which children have to match the same word written in different fonts. The children can make their own versions of these games while learning about different fonts and font sizes available on a computer.

- Use a computer to print labels in a variety of fonts. Focus on the differences between them. Which fonts would be most suitable for Violet, Mr Write and Word Bird?

- Use the picture of the Word Bird (magpie) on page 24. Ask the children to label the parts of the body ('beak', 'eyes', 'claws', and so on). Encourage them to use a dictionary to check the spellings of their labels.

- Make an interactive street frieze. Children can use cut-out labels to place appropriate signs on buildings. They can sort the signs into names and directions or warnings. They can also arrange them in alphabetical order.

- Model handwriting. Discuss how to join up different strings of letters, such as 'oo', 'est' and 'oy'. Explain how learning to write a letter-string can help with spelling.

A PCET poster, designed to be used in conjunction with all the above activities, is available from Channel 4 Schools. It displays a range of labels, including symbols, warning signs and food labels.

Writing a Rhyme

Programme outline

Mr Write realises that it will be soon his mum's birthday and that he needs to make a birthday card for her. Violet tells him to write a rhyme for the card. Through Word Bird's magic magpie eye, teen pop group Cleopatra explain how they use rhyme in their music. Mr Write makes a card and discusses how to make words rhyme. He and Violet play a game of rhyming snap before they send the card.

Before watching

- Find out what kinds of playground rhymes the children know. Do they have special actions? Ask the children to perform them.

While watching

- Stop after Word Bird has said 'Ah, Tuesday… Newsday'. What do the children notice about the sound of those words? Can they comment on the internal rhyme and the ending rhyme? Can they remember what word Violet used to rhyme with Monday?

After watching

(T) Text-level activities

- Discuss the rhymes that the children can remember from the programme, such as Word Bird's:

  Come and see what I can spy
  Through my magic magpie eye.

- Ask the children to remember the kinds of rhymes that appear in birthday cards. Sing the rhyme 'Happy birthday to you'.

- Collect cards for birthdays and other celebrations. Use the photocopier to enlarge the verses inside and ask children to highlight the words that rhyme. Discuss the presentation of the greeting in terms of style, print and layout. Are the styles different for boys' and girls' cards? What does the picture on the front of the card tell you about who bought the card, or for whom it is intended? Do the verses match the pictures?

Happy Birthday

- Discuss the rhymes suggested by Mr Write:

  Have a day full of fun,
  Play a game in the sun.

  Have a day full of treats,
  Lots of presents and sticky sweets.

  Have a day full of jellies,
  Jump in a puddle in your wellies.

- Working alone or in groups, children can make their own rhymes starting with 'Have a day full of…'

- Children can make up rhymes and design cards for different special occasions. What else needs to go on the card (greeting on the front, who it is to and from…)? How is the envelope addressed?

Sentence-level activities

- Enlarge Mr Write's poem on a flip chart and use it to discuss the layout of a rhyme.

  What cake
  Shall I bake?
  A magic cake
  Is what I'll make.

  Questions for discussion might include :

  - Why are the lines written one under another?
  - How do we notice the rhyming words?
  - Why does each line start with a capital letter?
  - What punctuation has been used?

- On an OHP transparency, copy Word Bird's rhyming couplets about cats on page 25. Talk with the children about rhyme, rhythm and punctuation.

- Write out a 'days of the week' rhyme, such as 'Today's Monday', with no capital letters. Ask the children to write in the correct capital letters using a pen of another colour. Draw their attention to the fact that the names of the days of the week are proper nouns and require a capital letter.

- Consider the layout of birthday cards and cards for other celebrations. Read the printed message and point out where a personal message can be written. Make a collection of cards and envelopes to be used for models to teach the use of capital letters for personal names and street and place names.

- Demonstrate how to address a letter.

Word-level activities

- Invite the children to recite rhymes, such as Solomon Grundy, for days of the week. Discuss the order of the days of the week. As a shared writing activity, make a list of the days of the week, discussing how they are spelt. Make a collection of published rhymes and stories that use the days of the week, such as *Jasper's Beanstalk*, *The Hungry Caterpillar*, or *Monday's Child* from *Clever Polly and the Stupid Wolf*.

- As a shared writing activity, make up rhyming words for each day of the week. For example: *Monday-Bunday, Tuesday-Newsday, Wednesday-Pensday*. Children individually can make zig-zag books to illustrate a week in rhyme.

- Using Violet's 'Hickory Dickory Dock' rhyme as a starting point, explore rhyming words for numbers up to ten. Distinguish between rhymes that have similar spelling patterns and those that do not. For example:

  one: fun, sun, run, ton, won
  two: few, blew, chew, stew, blue, flew
  three: me, tree, see, bee, knee, tea, sea

- Select some of the rhymes with common letter strings (such as *three*, *tree*, *see*) as a basis for modelling handwriting joins and for helping children learn spelling patterns.

- Mr Write's birthday message was a near-miss rhyme: 'mum' and 'fun' *nearly* rhymed:
  To a very lovely mum
  Have a birthday full of fun.
  Discuss the similarity between the 'm' and 'n' sounds. Ask children to suggest other words to rhyme or nearly rhyme with 'mum'.

- Discuss how 'birthday' is made up of two words: 'birth' and 'day'. Discuss how other compound words, such as 'teapot', 'football', 'handbag', 'playground' or 'sunflower', can be split. Children can make up a matching-pairs game using the two halves of compound words. Can they make real and imaginary words from them?

A birthday cat – now that's absurd! A cat on a card is not for this bird.

A PCET poster, designed to be used as a teaching resource and to support children's independent work in conjunction with the above activities, is available from Channel 4 Schools. It illustrates different styles of cards for special occasions, with a particular focus on rhyme.

Writing Instructions

Programme outline

Mr Write is reading the book *Jim and the Beanstalk*. He decides he wants to grow some beans too. Word Bird shows us how, in real life, a gardener follows instructions for growing. Back in the house, Mr Write learns how to write a set of instructions for growing beans, and makes them into a book. Violet shows how to follow instructions to paint a magic picture; and Mr Write performs his own bit of magic to rustle up some beans for tea. The only problem is – they are in cans!

Before watching

- If possible, make a collection of stories which involve growing things, such as *Jim and the Beanstalk*, *Jasper's Beanstalk* and traditional versions of *Jack and the Beanstalk*.

- Ask the children about any instructions they have encountered during the day: for example, spoken ones such as 'Get up and have a wash', 'Hurry up, you'll be late for school', 'Stop talking', 'Put your books away'; or written ones such as 'Open here', 'Now wash your hands', 'Only two people allowed in the sand pit'.

- Make a list of all the other types of instructions that children can think of or find around them. Can they be sorted into different types, such as those that explain things to us or those that tell us what to do?

While watching

- Stop the video after Violet has told Mr Write 'You need to write some instructions', and he replies 'Instructions?' Can the children explain to Mr Write what instructions are? Can they refer back to any examples of instructions that they have already seen in the programme? Resume the video to hear what Violet explains to him.

After watching

 **Text-level activities**

- Discuss the instructions that Mr Write used to grow his beans, focusing on the language and tone of them. As a shared writing activity, compose instructions for growing beans. Consider the audience, the information that needs to be given, and the order of the instructions. Discuss the use of annotated diagrams to facilitate understanding.

- Enlarge instructions on seed packets for use in shared reading activities. Discuss any symbols or diagrams used. Discuss how the writing is impersonal and direct, without using pronouns, so that instead of 'You put the seeds...' the writer directly instructs the gardener to 'Put the seeds...'.

- Children could cut out flower pictures from catalogues or magazines to make their own seed packets, carefully writing out the instructions they think will be needed. Talk about how the inclusion of labelled diagrams may make writing the instructions easier.

- As a shared writing activity, ask children to compose instructions for growing beans, or making porridge, a cup of tea, a fruit salad or a sandwich. Discuss how numbers are used to help sequence events. (See 'Sentence-level activities' below.) Choose a sample of their instructions and try following them. Were there any instructions missing? Was the sequencing all right? Were they easy to follow?

  Ask children to select activities from their lives to sequence and write instructions for – such as brushing teeth, laying the table, getting dressed.

- Encourage children to grow their own beans using blotting paper and transparent containers. Get them to record in words and pictures the progress of their beans' growth. They could make their records into a book, just as Mr Write did.

Sentence-level activities

- In Mr Write's bean-growing book, he doesn't use punctuation at the end of his statements. Talk with the class about when to use full stops, and ask them to explain to Mr Write when and why he should use a full stop.

- Use the instructions in the programme and those written by the class as a basis for revising the use of capital letters for headings and the beginning of sentences, and full stops at the end of sentences. Point out and discuss how numbers are sometimes used to help sequence instructions. Numbers can help the writer to think about the logical sequencing of what they write and help the reader understand the instructions by dividing the information into manageable chunks.

- As a shared writing session, retell the story of Jack and the Beanstalk in a story-map format. Label and number each key event, showing the sequence of the story with arrows. Emphasise the use of capital letters for

the beginning of sentences and proper nouns, and the use of full stops at the end of sentences. Children can then use this story-map as a model for sequencing and labelling their own favourite stories, as an individual activity.

Word-level activities

- As a development from discussions while watching, ask the children to make a list of the rhyming words generated from those in the programme, such as 'soil'-'oil'-'boil'-'foil' or 'seed'-'weed'-'need'. Give examples showing the distinction between onset and rime, and ask the children to use felt pens to highlight the onsets and rimes in their word collections.

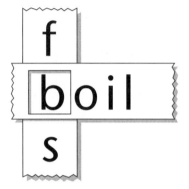

- Use the letter strings 'oil' and 'eed' to model handwriting joins and to teach spelling.

- Mr Write looks up the word 'water' in the dictionary. Can the children say where in the dictionary it would come? Ask them to find the word 'water' in a dictionary themselves.

  As a shared writing activity, put the words 'soil', 'pot', 'seed', 'water', 'plant', 'stem' and 'leaf' into alphabetical order. Where would the children find each of these words in the dictionary?

- As a shared writing activity, make a list of the basic parts of a plant: for example, 'seed', 'root', 'stem', 'leaf', 'flower'. As an independent activity, ask children to draw and label their own plant.

Speech Bubbles

Programme outline

Violet's photos have arrived. They show Mr Write and Violet having a fun day out in the park. Word Bird suggests that Mr Write add some speech bubbles to the photos, as in a comic strip. Word Bird takes us to meet the writer Jan Fearnley to see how she uses speech bubbles in her book *Mabel and Max*. Back in the Writing House, Mr Write and Word Bird discuss what they might be saying in the photos before writing some speech bubbles to stick on. Violet has the idea of using the photos to make a story with speech. The episode closes with Mr Write and Violet writing 'goodbye' on real balloons!

Before watching

■ Ask the children if they read any comics. Which are their favourite comics and characters? Can they comment on any particular features of a comic strip, such as speech bubbles, or the way the action within the picture takes the place of the words of the story?

While watching

■ Pause the programme and look at a close-up of the writer's work. How is the story being told? Encourage the children to observe the interaction between words and pictures. Notice how dialogue is written in the speech bubbles while the storyline is written below the pictures.

After watching

(T) **Text-level activities**

■ Talk with the class about how the writer worked. Why did she use speech bubbles? Discuss how Violet's photographs were used for storyboarding and how suitable speech bubbles were composed.

■ Carefully select an appropriate comic strip to enlarge and use as a text for shared reading. Discuss how the speech bubbles are used as an integral element of the storytelling. Extend this activity into shared writing: blank out the speech bubbles and ask the children to compose alternatives.

■ As a shared activity, make a story-map depicting the key elements and structure of a well-known story. Use appropriate speech bubbles to show the characters' motivation and response at key moments of the story shown on the map.

a story-map

Once modelled, this activity could be developed as an independent activity where children map their favourite story in a similar way, using words and pictures. In the plenary session, discuss how different children may have depicted the same story in different ways. Discuss the nature of our individual responses and how they are influenced by our life and previous reading experiences.

- As an independent activity, fold an A4 sheet of paper into eight sections to use as a storyboard for a well-known story such as *Little Red Riding Hood*, to include speech bubbles.

- Storyboard an imaginary animal or science-fiction story into eight sections using drawings and speech bubbles only. Then write out the story, transferring the speech bubbles into text using speech marks.

- Use photographs from a class outing or a class project to make up a storyboard similar to the one made by Violet in the programme. Compose suitable speech bubbles to accompany them.

- As a shared writing activity, model the first two pages of a book of excuses that a child gives their parent for not eating their vegetables, going to bed, or doing their homework. Use speech bubbles to write the dialogue between the child and the parent. Think of a different excuse for each day of the week.

Sentence-level activities

- Discuss the use of capital letters and exclamation marks for emphasis in speech bubbles.

- Using comics or books such as *Farmer Duck* and *This is the Bear*, explore and note how speech bubbles are used, the way the words are written and the use of punctuation. Talk about how the punctuation can affect the delivery of the lines. Discuss the need for brevity and the impact of a message within the limited space of a speech bubble.

- This activity can be developed for independent work: children can animate their pictures by adding speech and thought bubbles generated on a word processor. Children can be introduced to drawing boxes and shapes around their text, as well as considering the style and size of the text used. Do different fonts suit different characters?

- Use extracts from popular books as examples to further examine and model the use of speech marks in dialogue.

- As a shared writing activity, consider and then compose what various children and adults in the playground might say. Invite the children to suggest how speech bubbles could be used to record their dialogue. Introduce the use of capital letters, exclamation marks, bold type and so on as indicators of emphasis.

- Make a large playground frieze using children's drawings and suggestions with the speech bubbles stuck on. The speech bubbles can be produced on a word processor using a range of sizes and fonts.

Using the speech bubbles of the playground frieze as a starting point, ask children to write a very short scene between two or three characters – for example, an argument over a skipping-rope. Discuss how to extract the dialogue from the speech bubbles, and encourage them to write it using speech marks.

Word-level activities

- Collect single words or short phrases that are commonly written in speech bubbles in comics, such as 'Help' or 'Stop'. Discuss the use of onomatopoeic words such as 'Brrr!', 'Eek!' 'Ahhh!' and 'Phew!' Consider how they are spelled, and list them to form a word bank for future work.

- Mr Write noticed and commented upon 'ust' words: 'just', 'must', 'rust'. Use these to model diagonal handwriting joins. Extend the activity to make analogies with other spellings (such as 'rusty', 'trust', 'crust', 'custard', 'justice'. Use a rhyming dictionary to demonstrate how to supplement the children's word lists.

Writing a Recipe

Programme outline

Mr Write, Violet and Word Bird have each invited a surprise guest to The Writing House for tea. They need to prepare a special recipe. Word Bird shows us how a professional chef uses recipes, and we see how a pizza is made. Back at the Writing House, Violet and Mr Write make things easier by writing out the recipe before Mr Write rustles up his special meal. The surprise guest arrives – and what a surprise: everyone has invited the same person! It is the athlete Ben Challenger, Commonwealth Games silver medallist.

Before watching

- Ask the children if they have ever sent or received an invitation. Ask them what occasion it was for.

- Discuss the sort of food they like to eat on special occasions or when a friend is coming to their home for tea.

While watching

- Pause the programme after Violet has shown her email. Explain electronic mail to the children, and how quickly messages can be sent and received using this service, compared with the postal system. Ask children to comment on their own experience of email.

- Stop the programme after the pizza has been made. Ask the children what ingredients were used and how it was made.

After watching

(T) Text-level activities

- Display a good selection of recipe books for children to browse through. Allow them the opportunity to discuss with each other which recipes appeal to them and why.

- Have a range of cookery books for children to study. Look at the variety of layouts and uses of illustration. Which do children prefer? Why?

- Discuss the different components of a recipe: the list of ingredients and utensils, the sequence of instructions, and the use of annotated illustrations.

- As a stimulus for writing, children can make their own simple pizzas, using small squares of ready-made pizza base or slices of bread. Provide a selection of toppings from which children can choose. Cook the pizzas.

- Children can make individual zig-zag books to describe, in a non-narrative format, the stages of making a pizza. They can add photographs of their pizza.

- Discuss how the ingredients change with cooking. As a shared writing activity, record the effects of heat on food in a non-narrative format. Consider the language used, and its direct, impersonal style.

- Using the names they invent during sentence-level activities (see opposite), children can create imaginary recipe cards. They can either keep to conventional ingredients and methods or invent fantastical ones.

- Make a collection of printed, computer-published and handwritten invitations for the children to look at and use as a basis for discussion. For example, they could consider how the style and presentation reflect the nature of the occasion.

- As a shared writing activity, list the kinds of details that need to be written on an invitation. Compose a party invitation together as a model from which children can compose their own as an independent writing activity. This could be extended to include the use of a computer to design and publish the invitation incorporating pictures and text.

- Demonstrate how to address an envelope, so that children can address their own invitations.

(S) Sentence-level activities

- Violet had written 'RSVP' on her invitation. Discuss what this means, and the purpose of abbreviations in general. List some other abbreviations that the children may be familiar with, such as CITV, CBBC, WC, AA, RAC, RSPCA, BT. Discuss the use of capital letters. Ask children to write their initials as capital letters.

- Make a collection of invitation cards and reply cards. Consider the key words and phrases, any abbreviations used, and the layout of the cards. Talk about where the capital letters and full stops are needed.

- Revise the use of capital letters for the days of the week.

- Ask the children to describe Mr Write's recipe card. As a shared writing activity, write out the recipe for rice and peas, paying attention to the layout, the language, and the use of capital letters and full stops.

- Children could create names for fantastical recipes for special occasions, such as 'Fizzy, Wizzy Whirls' for Bonfire Night, or 'Heart's Delight' for Valentine's Day. Discuss the use of capital letters for names and titles. On a computer, try different fonts and print out the version that seems best suited to the occasion.

(W) Word-level activities

- As a shared writing activity, make a list of all the toppings used on pizzas, such as tomatoes, cheese, ham, mushrooms, pineapple, pepperoni, peppers, sweetcorn, onion... Sort the list into alphabetical order for use as a class resource. Working independently, the children can draw or paint a large pizza with all their favourite toppings on it, using the list to label all the toppings of their pizza.

- Extend Mr Write's list of 'ice' words ('rice', 'mice', 'nice') with other words such as 'dice', 'slice', 'spice', 'twice', 'price', 'advice', 'device'. Use these words to model handwriting joins and for spelling practice. Broaden the list to include other words that have the same string of letters but different pronunciations, such as: 'notice', 'justice', and 'police'.

- Talk about Mr Write's strategies for finding words he was unsure of, such as using the recipe book for the word recipe, or reading the word 'coconut' from the tin. What strategies can the children think of for finding words they don't know?

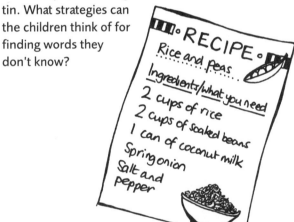

- As a shared writing activity, make a list of cooking verbs, such as 'wash', 'cut', 'chop', 'put', 'place', 'spread', 'stir', 'mix', 'pour', 'boil', 'simmer', 'grill', 'bake', 'cook', 'add'... Sort the list into alphabetical order to use as a resource for recipe writing.

- Discuss other words they may need when writing their recipes such as 'first', 'next', 'then', 'after'...

A PCET poster is available to stimulate and support discussion and further work on the topic of instructions. It displays the recipe for making pizza, and offers a basic model for sequencing and layout which children can adapt to meet their own needs.

Describing a Character

Programme outline

Violet has received her first letter from her penfriend Meena in India. Meena has written all about herself, and wants to know all about Violet. Word Bird introduces us to 6-year-old Shoaib, who tells us all about his mum. Meanwhile, in the Writing House, Mr Write and Word Bird write some notes about Violet's character for her to use in her letter to Meena. They finish the letter together before Mr Write takes a photograph of Violet to send to Meena. The photograph does not come out well – so Meena will have to imagine what Violet looks like from her description.

Before watching

■ Ask the children to describe themselves or a friend. Encourage them to comment on more than just their physical appearance – such as what makes them happy, sad, or angry, their likes and their dislikes. What characteristics do we like the most in people? What attracts us to particular characters?

While watching

■ Stop the tape when the character chart for Violet is left for Mr Write and Word Bird to fill in. How would the children fill in the chart? What would they say about Violet?

After watching

(T) Text-level activities

■ Discuss the letter that Violet finally wrote to Meena and the way in which she described Mr Write and Word Bird (see page 26) – starting with what they are, what they look like, what they enjoy doing, how they behave and how they feel about things.

■ Use a well-known character from a story or nursery rhyme as a stimulus for a shared writing activity. Stick their picture or name on the centre of a flip chart and write all the children's comments on the character around it to create an annotated character study which includes descriptions of appearance, behaviour and personality.

■ Play the character game, in which a descriptive clue is given of a fairytale character – for example, for Snow White the clue might be 'I am the fairest of them all', 'I am friends with seven miners' or 'a witch poisoned me with an apple'. As a shared writing activity, write clues for another well-known character from a book.

This can be extended into an independent writing activity by giving children a 'lift the flap' task, where they draw their character on the bottom sheet and write clues about them on the top sheet. You could include characters like Little Red Riding Hood, Baby Bear or the Big Bad Wolf.

■ As an independent writing activity, children can make character sketches of themselves. Help them to structure their descriptions by listing their characteristics under the headings: 'what I look like', 'what I like doing' and 'what I am like' (how I behave and feel about things). This could be extended to include friends and family. These could be presented in a narrative form or as annotated drawings.

(S) Sentence-level activities

■ Use 'hotseating' to develop children's skills at asking and answering questions and to explore more fully the dimensions of story characters. For example, ask the children what they already know about Violet and record their comments. Then ask what they would like to find out about her and make a list of questions.

Children in the class can then volunteer to assume the character of Violet and answer the questions written down and any others that may occur as a result of the hotseating. The responses can be recorded in order to compile a more detailed character study of her. Has anyone changed their opinion of Violet?

- Using Violet's character sketch as a basis for a shared writing activity, make character sketches of Mr Write and Word Bird. Consider the composition of the descriptive sentences to be used; discuss grammatical agreement between verbs and pronouns, and the use of capital letters and full stops.

- At the end of her letter, Meena wrote a postscript introduced with the abbreviation 'PS'. Explain the use of 'PS' and link it with previous work on abbreviations.

ⓦ Word-level activities

- Mr Write noticed the 'ing' endings on the verbs when they were writing about what Violet likes doing: gardening, riding her bike and using the computer. As a shared writing activity, collect and list the things that the children like doing. Using a highlighter pen, ask children to come up to the flip chart and highlight any 'ing' endings that they notice.

- Discuss different verbs with similar meanings, or different ways of expressing preference, such as:

  I like riding my bike.
  I enjoy riding my bike.
  I love riding my bike.
  I am happy when I am riding my bike.
  My favourite hobby is riding my bike.

- As a shared writing activity, draw an outline of a well-known media character (for example, Donald Duck) and write one word or a short phrase that describes an attribute or characteristic of them. What would be the opposite of this characteristic? For example, two outlines of wolves could be drawn; inside one the words 'huge', 'mean', 'scary', 'cunning', 'greedy' could be written; inside the other the words 'thin', 'hungry', 'starving', 'timid', 'shy', 'polite'.

- As an extension, children could work in pairs using the same character in different moods: for example, a brave little pig and a scared little pig, a polite Goldilocks and a rude Goldilocks, a gentle giant and a cruel giant.

Some people think my mum is strange...

Some people think my mum is strange...

With her green and orange spiky hair,
Lots of glitter everywhere,
Purple eyes and bright blue lips,
Different-colour fingertips
And long, long, long, long earrings.

With her squeaky black leather jacket,
She really makes an awful racket.
Pink and yellow stripy shirt,
Shiny silver miniskirt
And big, big, big, big golden boots.

She always plays her loud guitar
Singing like a top pop star,
Always happy, never down,
Always smiling, never frowns,
And dancing, dancing round and round.

If she did all this alone at home
It wouldn't be so bad.
But she comes to school and plays the fool –
It nearly drives me mad.
But my class all think she's really ace,
The best they've ever had,
'Cos she's our teacher... that's my mum
And I'm really, really glad.

Paul Cookson

Questions

Programme outline

Mr Write is doing the animal crossword from his local paper. He loves animals and really wants a pet. Word Bird takes him, via his magic magpie eye, to a pet rescue centre. We see how questionnaires are used to help match the pets to the most suitable owners. Mr Write sees a dog he'd like. He writes to the pet centre with some questions about him. He drafts the letter by hand first, then Violet emails it to the pet centre. He gets a reply, and realises that there is more to looking after a dog than he had first thought. Violet and Word Bird save the day when they spot a notice asking for help with dog-walking. Mr Write is pleased – at least he will get a share of a pet dog.

Before watching

- Ask the children if they have pets, and if not, what pets they would like. How would they look after them? Invite children to ask each other questions about looking after their pets. Discuss the different needs of pets in terms of food, habitat and care routines.

While watching

- Pause the programme as Mark and his dad fill in the form. Ask the children what they already know about forms and the kinds of questions they ask. Explain the function of a questionnaire and ask the children why they think Mark's dad is filling in this form.

After watching

(T) Text-level activities

- Ask the children to recall the letter that Mr Write wrote to the pet centre. Prompt them to consider the kinds of questions he asked and how he wrote them. Why did he send his letter by email? Discuss children's experience of email and how they might use it in school. Show the examples on page 27.

- Discuss why Mr Write decided not to get a pet. Do children and their parents share similar feelings?

- Use children's knowledge of their own pets as a basis for devising a survey to find out about the most popular types of pets and how they are looked after. As a shared writing activity, discuss and formulate questions for your survey. Consider with the children the most appropriate methods of recording the data collected and how to present it.

- Work on questions could be developed further. Invite a pet owner or animal expert into class and devise a shared list of questions to be used for interviewing them. In addition, ask each child to write out one specific question to ask the guest and listen carefully to their answer. Afterwards the children can write out the question and the answer that the guest gave, and their records can be compiled as a class book.

- As group work, introduce question-and-answer games, such as 'Animal, Vegetable and Mineral' that will encourage children to pose explicit questions. The first player thinks, for example, of a tiger, and the others have to guess their animal by asking yes-or-no questions. What kinds of questions are most effective?

- As a class, the children can email letters to local animal welfare organisations to find out more about their animals. Ask them to consider what they know already and then focus on the questions they need to ask.

(S) Sentence-level activities

- Use the class discussions as a basis for modelling the writing of questions. Focus on the importance of using capital letters to start and question marks to finish.

- Consider Mr Write's letter. Focus on the address at the top of the letter; in particular the need for capital letters for the street, town and county names, and postcodes that use capital letters and numbers. Encourage children to practice writing their own addresses.

- In his letter Mr Write used questions which began with 'wh' words. Discuss how words such as 'what', 'where', 'when', 'which', 'who' and 'why' are used to begin questions.

  Revise the questions Mr Write asked: 'What does Bob eat?' 'Where can Bob sleep?' 'When does Bob need to walk?' As shared writing, list other questions, such as: 'What is the best food?' 'Why does he need walking so often?'

  As an individual activity, ask children to compose questions about looking after a pet, using 'wh' words.

- Read books that use questions repetitively (for example, *What's the time, Mr Wolf?* by Colin Hawkins). Use this as a stimulus for making a big-book alternative version (called, for example, *Where are you going Mr Wolf? To the bathroom to brush my teeth*). Use children's names to substitute in, for example, *Brown Bear, Brown Bear, what do you see?* so that it reads *Keranjit, Keranjit, what do you see? Sally in a red dress looking at me.* Focus on the use of question marks and revise work on capital letters.

Ⓦ Word-level activities

- At the beginning of the programme Mr Write tries out a crossword puzzle. Model the construction of crossword puzzles using the examples from the programme. As a shared writing activity, make a list of animals and construct a simple puzzle (or word chain) using four or five animals from the list. Make up clues to go with them. Demonstrate how blank squares represent the letters and how the clues are numbered.

  Working in pairs, some children may be able to construct their own puzzles on squared paper.

- Focus on the 'wh' words used by Mr Write to start his questions – 'what', 'where', 'when' – and link to other words beginning with 'wh', such as 'why', 'white', 'whale', 'wheel', 'whisper', 'whistle'. Look in a dictionary to see how many words begin with 'wh'. Mention that a long time ago people used to write 'wh' as 'hw', which represented an 'h' sound before a 'w' sound. Although the letters are now reversed to 'wh', people still retain a soft 'h' sound.

- Focus on the spelling of 'wh' question words. Model handwriting the letter string.

- Discuss other words that are useful for starting questions, such as 'how' and 'can'.

- Collect words that rhyme with, for example, 'eat', 'sleep' and 'walk', to make up simple rhyming couplets. Use a question-and-answer format to compose a short poem, such as:

  What does my cat eat?
  Biscuits as a special treat.
  Where does my cat sleep?
  Amongst the wool of a sheep.
  When does my cat walk?
  At midnight he will stalk.

- Collect words for ways of eating (such as 'munch', 'chew', 'nibble', 'bite'...), sleeping ('rest', 'nap', 'snooze'...), or moving ('run', 'stroll', 'race'...). Make up rhyming couplets to make into a poem, using different animals. You could try 'Who broke the cup and saucer?', 'Who spilt the lemonade?', 'Who fell from the slide?'

A PCET poster, available from Channel 4 Schools, illustrates how a pet survey could be designed, and models the style of questions that could be used to gather information. It can be used as a resource to support the above discussions and activities.

A Traditional Tale

Programme outline

Mr Write discovers his three old and rather dusty teddies. They remind Violet of the story of Goldilocks and the Three Bears. Neither Violet nor Mr Write can remember what happens in the story, so Word Bird shows them a performance through his magic magpie eye. He leaves before the end, so Mr Write makes up a new ending to the story. Violet types it up on a word processor and adds different endings – using the 'delete' key to show how easily writing can be changed. Mr Write completes his story and settles down to eat his porridge – only to discover that the clever little bears got there before him!

Before watching

- List all the traditional tales that the children know. Ask them how they know them. Are there different versions? Ask them to recall the best part of their favourite story. Do all the stories have elements of adventure and scary parts? Are there good and bad characters?

While watching

- After Violet has told them her ending to the story of Goldilocks and the Three Bears, pause the video and ask the children how they think Mr Write could end his story.

- When Violet is altering the text on the computer, pause the video and explain the keys on the computer keyboard and how the computer can be a useful tool for writing and editing.

After watching

(T) Text-level activities

- Discuss children's responses to Mr Write's story endings.

- Make simple finger or paper-bag puppets for children to re-enact and tell the story of Goldilocks and the Three Bears in their own way.

- In groups, ask the children to act out a section from a traditional tale, such as the bears coming home from their walk and finding the porridge eaten, the chairs broken, or Goldilocks asleep. How would they react; what would their facial expressions be; what would they be saying? Use the children's role play as a basis for rewriting the story in a shared writing session, incorporating the childrens' dialogue and descriptions of the characters' responses.

- Children can work in groups to write the opening and closing sentences of the same story. Use the plenary session to read their suggestions and decide as a class the most suitable choices. This activity can be extended by asking the children to retell the beginnings and endings of other well-known traditional tales.

- As an independent activity, provide a range of ready-made books and simple bookmaking materials as a stimulus for the children's writing. Children can design books in which to retell their own version of a traditional tale. Which version will they base it on – the video, the one their grandmother told them, or the story they have had read to them from a book?

- Word Bird drops a leaflet onto Mr Write's desk. What are leaflets for? How do they work? Ask the children to bring in junk mail from home. Choose one leaflet to use for shared reading and explore the information it gives.

What do the children think would have to be written on the leaflet that Word Bird gave to Mr Write? As a shared writing activity, design a leaflet. Talk about the information that needs to be given to the reader – for example: title of play, venue, time, price, and names of actors. Focus on the structure of the sentences and the use of capital letters. Discuss the layout and what needs to go on it. Use a computer to try out different layouts, colours and fonts.

Sentence-level activities

- As group work, set up a 'small world' play based on Goldilocks and the Three Bears. Provide writing materials and ask the children to label, for example, 'Daddy Bear's Bed' and 'Mummy Bear's Bowl'. Remind them of the need to use capital letters for their labels.

- Violet uses the cursor keys to correct her spelling mistake. Encourage children to write their stories on the computer and practise using the cursor keys to edit their work.

Word-level activities

- Violet makes a play on words using the homophones 'bear' and 'bare'. Discuss how these words are spelled. Make a list of other homophones and see if children can make up jokes using them. They may already know some. Try: 'hair' and 'hare'; 'stare' and 'stair'; 'blue' and 'blew'.

- Using the word 'back' as an example, make a list of words ending in 'ck', such as 'black', 'stack', 'sack', 'Jack', 'tick-tock', 'lick', 'brick'. Model the handwriting join for 'ck'.

- Focus closely on the spelling of 'Goldilocks'. What words can the children find in it? As a shared activity demonstrate how to find words within words – for example, 'ear' in 'bear', 'let' in 'Violet'…

- There are 'three' bears in the story. Can the children spell and write other numbers? What other stories and songs have numbers in them? Can they recall the titles – such as 'Five Green and Speckled Frogs'?

story/song	creature	number
Goldilocks	bears	three
Snow White	dwarves	seven

A set of posters is available to support this series of programmes, one of which demonstrates how to make a simple folded book. More experienced children could work independently, following the instructions.

Writing a Guidebook

Programme outline

Mr Write is tidying the Writing House in preparation for a visit from Mr Wonderwand, the most important magician in the world. It's a very special occasion for all the residents. In order to impress, he needs to prepare a guidebook so that Mr Wonderwand won't get lost in house. Using what he's learnt from Word Bird's visit to Chester Zoo, Mr Write prepares his own special report in a book using drawings and pictures. When Violet adds her computer-drawn plans, the book is complete.

Before watching

- Find out whether the children have made any visits to shopping centres or places of interest. How did they find their way around? Discuss the use of town plans, shop plans and guidebooks. If possible, have some examples to look at.

While watching

- Stop the tape after Violet suggests making a guidebook. What do the children think should go in a guidebook for the Writing House? What illustrations would they use?

After watching

(T) Text-level activities

- Ask the children to recall how Mr Write and his friends made their guidebook. Why did they need it? How did they use it? What is the importance of a contents page?

- As a shared writing activity, consider what you would need to put into a guidebook for use by visitors to the school. In pairs or groups, select sections to focus on. How would you describe each room to make a visitor want to go there? Make drawings or take photographs of specific features to go with your written work. Include a map for the book. Compile all the work in the best order and number the pages. Make a contents page for your guide.

- Collect a range of guidebooks for children to look at. What do they tell you about the places they describe? How do you know where to go? Do they all have a contents page? Ask children to work in groups or pairs to compare features of two guidebooks and make a list of similarities and differences between them – for example, is there is a contents page or map? does it give a history or description of the area? As a shared activity, compile what the children have found out. Which features did the children think were most useful and which features did they think least useful?

- As a shared writing activity, design one section of a guidebook for the school: for example, the library, toilets or classroom. Can the children compose a brief description of the room that will make a visitor want to see it?

The Writing House
by
Mr Write, Violet Plant
and
Word Bird

- Consider the wider environment. Invite the children to make a guidebook for the local area. It might include: where the visitor can post a letter; public transport; recreation facilities; safe places to cross the road.

⊕ Sentence-level activities

- Write a description such as that used by Mr Write.

- What sections need to be in the guidebook, and how many pages would be needed for each? Design a mock-up for a guidebook; work out the number of pages needed, and the balance between text, illustration and annotated diagrams and maps.

- Focus on the development of one section, such as the contents page. As an independent activity, get the children to research what a contents page can look like in different contexts. Ask them to suggest how the school guidebook contents page should be laid out, considering the audience that may read it.

  As a shared writing activity, draft the contents page, discussing in context the use of numbering, pictures, capital letters and full stops. Working independently or in pairs, the children can use a word processor to make up the contents page. Print it out in a range of fonts and after group discussion select the one most suitable to use for the guidebook. Ask the children to tell you where you need to put capital letters and full stops.

- As a shared writing activity, make a list of notices seen around the school or in the local environment, such as: 'Please wipe your feet'; 'Keep off the grass'; 'No ball games'. Revise the use of capital letters and full stops and exclamation marks.

  Working independently, children can use their word-processing skills to write notices for themselves or the classroom, choosing a suitable size and style of font.

⊛ Word-level activities

- Mr Write wrote 'Please tidy up' to remind Word Bird to tidy the turret. Discuss how messages would have a very different tone without words like 'please' and 'thank you' which emphasise politeness. Encourage children to think of strategies for remembering the spelling of these words, such as onset and rime, compound words, and words within words.

- Develop work on the school guidebook by encouraging the children to suggest adjectives to go with the things seen in each room that will entice the visitor to see the school, such as those used in Mr Write's book: 'There are also *exciting* books to read.' 'A *magnificent* magpie called Word Bird lives in a nest in the roof of the turret.' As a shared activity,

brainstorm a list of words, to use as a class resource. Encourage the children to suggest how to spell them and focus on specific spelling strategies, for example using prefixes or suffixes.

Mr Write noticed the 'oo' sound in 'roof', and added the words 'tooth' and 'hoof'. Ask children to extend this list with more words, such as 'proof'. Extend the list of words with a medial 'oo' sound to include other words such as 'fool', 'pool', 'cool' and 'stool'.

- Practise handwriting the 'oo' sound in letter strings such as 'oof', 'ooth', and 'ool', adding different onsets to these rimes.

A poster from PCET supports discussion and further work on the topic of descriptions. It displays a floor plan and a text extract from a guidebook about a school. It offers a good model for children's own report writing. There is also a dictionary poster and book-making poster.

A Fantasy Story

Programme outline

Mr Write is feeling poorly. Violet suggests he should read a story to cheer himself up. He enjoys reading fantasy stories; but unfortunately he has already read the book Violet chooses for him. He is persuaded to make up a fantasy story of his own. Word Bird's magic eye shows us how a class of children make up their ideal story. Fired with enthusiasm, Violet and Mr Write plan their own fantasy story. A game of consequences gives them lots of ideas for another story, and Mr Write is soon feeling better.

Before watching

■ Ask children about their favourite stories. What do they like about them? Help them to analyse the story in terms of character, setting, plot, and ending: Who were the main characters? Where was the story set? What was the story about? What happened in the end? Talk about what makes a story a fantasy.

While watching

■ Stop the tape after Mr Write has read out most of his monster story and Violet says it needs an ending. Ask the children for suggestions on how Mr Write could end his story.

After watching

(T) **Text-level activities**

■ Were any of the children's suggestions similar to Mr Write's? Can the children retell the story that Mr Write made up? Can they remember how it started? – 'In a classroom far away lived a tiny green monster...'

■ Demonstrate how to play a consequences-type game.

Get children to play the game in groups. Encourage them to be bold and imaginative; stress the humorous nature of the resultant sentences. Ask them to read out the finished sentences and complete them with drawings to make a humorous class book.

The giant in the Writing House ate the pineapple chunks

■ Make a list of story starting-points to compile as a class resource. Notice specific spelling features. Use one or two for practising handwriting – such as: 'Long, long ago...'; 'Once upon a time...'; 'In a distant land...'; 'Deep in space...'.

■ Encourage children to make brief plans for a story, using a table like the one below.

Characters	Setting	Plot	Ending
Cunning Cat and Daring Dog On the cliff at the seaside.		Daring Dog falls off a ledge trying to get a stick.	Cat uses a cunning trick to come to the rescue.
Peter and Ravinder	A haunted house.	They open a creaking door to a room and find a sobbing girl ghost.	They help her find her lost locket which will enable her to join her friends and family.

- Revise work on character descriptions from the programme. Encourage children to flesh out their characters by describing their physical appearance, likes and dislikes, and personality. As a shared writing activity, compose and compile some brief character descriptions. Using their story plans, children can write out their story, adding atmosphere and tension as needed and including speech and noises as necessary.

S Sentence-level activities

- Mr Write's monster lives in a little drawer in the classroom. As shared writing, make a list of other places where a monster might live, using Violet's description as a model: 'It likes dark places so I think it lives in a drawer in a classroom.' Get the children to think about where a monster might like to live, and why. Encourage them to tell you where to put capital letters and full stops: 'It likes noisy places so it lives in the back of the television in the sitting room.' 'It likes damp places so it lives in the plug hole of the bath.' 'It likes shiny places so it lives in a tin foil dish at the back of the kitchen cupboard.'

- As an independent activity, children can write a brief description of where their monster lives underneath their monster pictures.

- Use Mr Write's fantasy story on page 28 for punctuation practice, as a shared activity. All the capital letters, full stops and commas are missing. Discuss where the punctuation could go. More experienced writers may attempt this independently. As shared writing, compile the finished sentences of the consequences game (see page 22) into a chart, noting capital letters and full stops.

- As another shared writing activity, children can compose a short imaginative story. Make reference to grammatical agreements of tenses. Mr Write's story is written in the past tense.

- The children may need to add speech or 'noises' to their stories. Revise work on speech marks, exclamation marks and font styles to show how speech and sounds may be emphasised.

W Word-level activities

- Draw a monster or space alien, according to children's suggestions, and label the features in the way Violet did: 'It's a green monster with four arms, three eyes and pointed teeth.' Add adjectives and similes to enhance the descriptions, such as 'four', 'long', 'scaly arms', 'three', 'enormous purple eyes', 'pointed teeth', 'sharp as daggers'. As an independent activity children can draw their own labelled monster.

- Make a list of animals for animal fantasy stories. Ask children to point out specific features or aids to help spell them, such as the 'ph' and 'ant' in 'elephant'. Children can make up alliterative names for them, and they could suggest characteristics of the animal – for example: 'Extra-terrestrial Elephant', 'Sneaky Snargle', 'Digger Dog', 'Munching Monkey'. They could extend to alliterative sentences, such as: 'Extra-terrestrial Elephant eats Easter eggs eagerly.'

- Compile a list of settings for fantasy stories, such as: a forest, a lake, a football pitch, an unknown planet, the street, a playground, a haunted house, a bus, a beach…

- As shared writing, list words that would suit a specific genre of story. Use the list as a resource for children's own fantasy story-writing and to focus on spelling such as:

Fairy Story	Science Fiction
princess	astronaut
dragon	space suit
castle	spaceship
knight	mission control
sword	blast off
key	planet
horse	oxygen

- Mr Write mistyped the word 'school'. As shared writing, compile a list of 'ool' words such as 'school', 'tool', 'fool', 'stool'. Add other 'oo' words such as 'soon', 'balloon', 'spoon'.

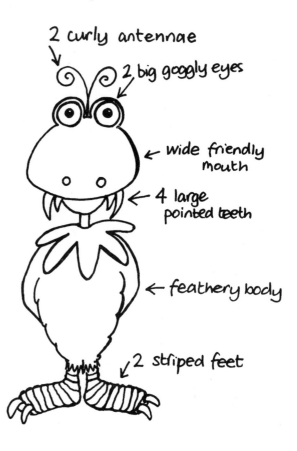

2 curly antennae

2 big goggly eyes

← wide friendly mouth

← 4 large pointed teeth

← feathery body

2 striped feet

Word Bird

How many parts of Word Bird can you label?

© 1999 CHANNEL FOUR LEARNING

Oh no, not a cat!

Word Bird is scared of cats. In each programme he makes up a rhyme about his feelings.

Programme 1   Cat! Oh no, don't say that word!
              Shut up! You know it scares this bird!

Programme 2   A birthday cat, now that's absurd.
              A cat on a card is not for this bird.

Programme 3   'A cat', up shout!
              Hey! Paint that out.

Programme 4   A cat's no laugh, I'd rather cry.
              You read for fun, I'll say bye-bye.

Programme 5   What a scary thought – a cat for tea!
              Forget the cakes, it might eat me!

Programme 6   You know that cats are what I fear –
              Cat's a word I hate to hear.

Programme 7   Aargh! A cat and a bird – why, that's absurd!
              A bird and a cat – we can't have that.

Programme 8   A fairy story about a cat –
              I don't want to hear a story like that.

Programme 9   Aargh! No, not that word, it drives me bats!
              When will you learn? I'm scared of cats.

Programme 10 A cat that's super, please – not that!
              Keep them at home, sat on a mat!

© 1999 CHANNEL FOUR LEARNING

9 Word Way
Pencilton
PP1 XX2

Dear Meena,

Thank you for your letter. I was very excited to receive it. I have written about my friends Mr Write and Word Bird and have asked them to help me write about myself.

Mr Write is a very good magician. He is tall and wears glasses. He likes practising his tricks as well as reading and writing. He is a bit messy and often forgets things but he is very friendly.

Word Bird is a magpie who lives with Mr Write at the Writing House. He has black and white feathers and a beak. He collects shiny objects and likes going on adventures. He is very funny, but sometimes is scared, especially when he sees a cat.

I am small and have blonde hair and blue eyes. I have sent you a photo so you can see exactly what I look like. I like riding my bike every day to the Writing House, where I enjoy gardening. Mr Write and Word Bird say I am helpful. I am also very tidy and quite a smiley, happy person. I don't have a pet but maybe one day I will get one.

Please write soon and tell me some more about yourself. Do you like football, and do you have a favourite team?

Love from
Violet

© 1999 CHANNEL FOUR LEARNING

Questions

```
=====================================================

From: Mr Write <mrwrite@writehouse.co.uk>
To: Pet Rescue Centre
<pencilton@rescuecentre.co.uk>
Date: 17 May, 10.34
Subject: Bob the dog

Dear Pet Centre

What does Bob eat?
Where can Bob sleep?
How many walks does Bob need?

Thank you

Mr Write


=====================================================

From: Pet Rescue Centre
<pencilton@rescuecentre.co.uk>
To: Mr Write <mrwrite@writehouse.co.uk>
Date: 17 May, 11.56
Subject: Re: Bob the dog

Dear Mr Write,

Bob should eat three tins of dog food a day.

You will have to remember to feed him every single
day.

Bob can sleep in the kitchen.

Bob needs to have a walk four times a day.

From Pencilton Pet Centre.
```

© 1999 CHANNEL FOUR LEARNING

monster in the class

in a classroom far away lived a tiny green monster who had four arms three eyes and sharp pointed teeth it liked the dark and lived inside a drawer

the monster loved to help the children with their writing and played tricks on them every day the children fed the monster on books especially adventure books which were a real treat

but one day they decided to give the monster a school dinner it was horrible the monster was very sick and turned bright orange

it was so scared that the children would give it another school dinner that it ran away and was never seen again

© 1999 CHANNEL FOUR LEARNING